LATELY

Stephen Yeo

Printed edition:
Also available in multiple e-book formats.

Published by:
The Endless Bookcase Ltd,
Suite 14 STANTA Business Centre, 3 Soothouse Spring,
St Albans, Hertfordshire, AL3 6PF, UK.

More information can be found at:
www.theendlessbookcase.com

Copyright © 2023 Stephen Yeo
All rights reserved.

The cover photograph, *Henry Moore's hands* by Gemma Levine shows the sculptor holding found objects in the Bourne Maquette Studio in 1978. Reproduced by kind permission of Tate Images www.tate-images.com, © Gemma Levine Archive at the Tate.

ISBN: 978-1-914151-76-7

Alongside his poems, Stephen Yeo has published widely in the fields of co-operative, religious, voluntary, labour and socialist association. After teaching social history at the University of Sussex, he became Principal of Ruskin College, Oxford and Chair of the Manchester-based Cooperative College and of the Trust which looks after the Pioneers' Museum in Rochdale and the National Co-operative Archive. As a founder of QueenSpark Books in Brighton, he helped to bring into being the Federation of Worker Writers and Community Publishers (FWWCP).

ACKNOWLEDGEMENTS

So many people have shown me how a poem cannot grow, shrink or wither until sounded in more than an empty room.

First and foremost: Ursula Howard. Many of the poems collected here would never have seen daylight, let alone be kept, without her uncommon sense, eye for detail and belief during times when I lost it.

Familial poets risk a lot from generation to generation, while their immediate families live with endless writerly preoccupations. Eileen Janes Yeo, our sons Jake and Ben – and now their families – helped me more than they will ever know, as did my late brother, Peter Yeo.

Fellow poets have been generous with their time and skill, particularly Fiona Sampson, Bernard O'Donoghue, Philip Gross, Merryn Williams, Ruth O'Callaghan, Jenny Lewis, Carole Baldock and Jane Spiro. Writers are competitive, yes, but in equal measure co-operative. Lauren Rusk, David Constantine, Carole Satyamurti, Clare Brant, Lucy Newlyn and Stephen Stuart-Smith all supported the project at key moments. So did Tamar Yoseloff, Robert Vas Dias, Sean O'Brien and members of workshops in London, Oxford, and at the Arvon Foundation. John O'Halloran, Jonathan Rée, Elisabeth Salisbury, Wyn Bramley, Meryem Kalayci, Kate McLoughlin and Marie Bridge have each been helpful readers.

Unless the editors of Poetry Review, Agenda, The Interpreter's House, Orbis, The New Humanist, Oxford Magazine, The Ringing World, QueenSpark, Isis, South-East Arts Review, Ruskin Writing, Friends Quarterly and The Friend, as well as the runner-up prize givers for the Keats-Shelley, and the annual Poetry Review best uncollected poet prize (presented to me by Peter Porter) ...unless these generous souls had 'taken' my work as they did, I would have given up, with the compost heap as the sole beneficiary.

Rummaging into his living, the poet fetches
The images out that hurt and connect
    W.H.Auden, December 1938

    Our hurts unclinching
    As we become more akin

    To kin, as we return
    To who we were
    Amanda Gorman, *Back to the Past*, 2021.

CONTENTS

Because 1

1. GODSENDS AND SILENCES

Lover 5
Winter Walk 6
Persevera 7
Zion 9
Plasma 10
Taking A View 12
A Sea That May Go On Some Time 15
List Of Work 1902 16
From A China Diary, 1988 17
Yet Franciscan Don 25
Little Boys 28
Newborn 31

2. TRIBUTES AND ACHES

Thank You, Auden 34
Meditation In Unseasonal Haiku 38
Passion Flower 39
Sister Future Perfect 40
Incarnation 41
Shakescene 46
Invitation To A Dead Heading 47
Where There Only Ever Is 48
How Are We Supposed To Sing? 49
The Violet Ray Machine 52
Time To Move On 53
Poet Learns To Get Lost 54
A Christmas Gospel 57
Instructions From Los 58
Poetry 59
A Part Of Speech? 60
Fresh Green Sap 61

3. LIST AND FOUND NOW AND THEN

Folie De Grandeur 64
Painter 65
In- Habited 66
An Illicit Ache 67
Parenthesis 68
Ezekiel 69
Now And Then 70
Endearments 71
His Daughter To Her Daughter 74
Though He Could 75
Muse To Poet 76
'god' 77
Complications 78
Another Ache 80
Epithalamium 82
Grandfather 83
Lover, Again 84
Yes, But… 85
Envoi 86

Notes and Debts 88

BECAUSE

A void exists
chameleon,
until we limn it.

The truth lies
harlequin,
until we
       ĕlēē ´mŏsÿnarÿ
hymn it.

1.

GODSENDS AND SILENCES

LOVER
for Ursula

Yours a honeysuckle, once *woodbine*.
Mine: Lorna Doone, Citrus White, Fur Leaved, wild and hybrid thyme.
Yours the whiteness of chalked green, lilies of the valley.
Mine Salmon Dream, a peony.

Yours – white mock-orange – sugared our summer.
Mine, a quickening scent – broad beans – not quite vanilla.
Yours a bearded-iris bed. Would that
I, solitary bee, could fly, feed, come clumsily out.

Ours is… a love (in-a-mist), seedpods, elf-like nigella,
clematis, aquilegia, self-sown
primroses, heartsease …that goldfinch nest seen through a field-gate.
Do you remember, how she never came home?

WINTER WALK

sing winter solstice in
while starlings shriek
on leafless trees

December days
in middle age
and bitter times

such moments fall
and then they fall
on sheep as maggots

high on grazing land
red thorn-bush berries
make scars on Hadrian's Wall

so pick them out with song
which will go wrong
in three days' time

as Christians sing too timidly
in liturgies
which hide the blood

PERSEVERA - PER SEVERA - PERSE||VERA

Peals

Grandsire Triples
Grandsire Caters
Stedman Triples
Stedman Caters
Stedman Cinques
Union Triples
College Single Triples
Bob Major
Bob Royal
Double Oxford Major
Double Norwich Major
Duffield Major
Oxford Treble Bob Major
Kent Treble Bob Major
Kent Treble Bob Royal
Kent Treble Bob Maximus
Duffield Royal
Superlative Surprise Major

> There's plenty to be said about stressed and unstressed syllables and the stressed and unstressed writers who count them up, but the important question (for me) is whether you hear …a hurrying, incremental kind of music or whether you hear something more to and fro and rewinding like birdsong *Alice Oswald, introducing Thomas Wyatt's poems.*

and Changes

upon the campanological side
carelessness leaves bells high up
some windy inaccessible tower un-
visited save by owls and jackdaws
precarious ladders, dangerous steps

after two hours the long draught at Totnes
made the 7th and tenor unpealable
at Exeter Stedman Caters came to
grief the seven front bells inaudible
to strangers unaccustomed to the belfry

many failures follow due in each case to
bells not ringers at Saint Finbar's Fowey
the bad go of the bells entangled ropes
made even call-changes impossible
at Kenwyn Superlative Surprise failed.

ZION

On the face of Arizona
winter sun shines
in green brush-sage
Joshua trees
succulents and cacti.

Mesquite
many-coloured coral from a desert sea
with pale blue juniper berries
exist

as dry –
then dried by riverene, Pima Indians –
as Arizona Queen of the Night
Peniocerus Gregii,
and wild Ponderosa pines
are delicate.

American Dippers
John Muir's favourite bird
and mine
will bob on stones:

dip, dip, dip
in the Virgin River
never missing
toeholds in the waters of Zion.

You, they will say in Phoenix,
have a good day.

Walk, a signal says
Walk. On the Light.

PLASMA

Surprisingly often
a She but sometimes
an It, corn-king boat
flood omen thunderbolt
or coincidental
sign of Otherness
comes, occurs, descends
as caesura | dis-
continuity
apocalyptic
break or commandment
to climb on board –
not half telling, with
less than half showing.

In Christendom It
took flesh as a Him
a three in one He
who, like all sacred
or secular mavens,
came from somewhere un-
known, claiming foreknowledge
of what he had come to:
a place where most things
that would happen | hadn't,
and most things that should
come (to pass) would never,
until His Big Other's
story was heard.

From holy lands
between east and now
The West, we sent him
(lower case now) back
with a flea in his ear.
Kill, kill! Tortured, nailed
to two hard planks, hands
first, feet crossed | hammered.
Mocked: *try some vinegar*,
speared, *look at your water*.
For not being – what?
A master key which
was him uncut? King
Lud? An act of God?

Ever since then we
generate prophets
watch crab-apples fall
kiss statues in marble
stick needles in wax
fall ill with mania
rehearse revolution
compose reminders:
Recordare Iesu pie...
I AM | the cause you
came for. *Drink this, eat*.
We cover the world
with bodies and blood
claim yours, as plasma.

TAKING A VIEW

*People don't look, they scan the ground in front of them
to check there's nothing in the way,*
David Hockney, January 2012

1.

A single, external point of view, fixed
with vanishing point, *means that you, the viewer
aren't there. You aren't moving, you're dead*
no longer part of your own picture.

Renaissance perspective is *violent.*
Invisible, wing-shitting killers –
bombers – use it on camera: insurgent
X to Ype. Zap: a catalogue of terror.

He stole *eye fuck* - Vietnam G.I abuse -
to edge us in to look, walk eye to eye
in Woldgate Woods seeing every season
the process of looking is the beauty.

We're lumps of stuff, not mathematical points.

2.

En plein aire, the world as theatre
or scroll, *cubism of the brush*. A fax
of a picture of a mother in a mirror
in colour, from an app and a printer,

tarmacadam as matt or (can't be?) mauve,
'wet' for rain, white ideograms for drops,
leaves as light bulbs, more singular than Claude's.
Heart, eye and hand, his joined-up marks

dance to the physic of colour seeing
with memory, us in, here now, there then,
back to front he catches the eye's mind singing
trees in twelve-tone shades of summer green.

YOU move, seeing both sides of the object.

3.

If painting like poetry 'makes nothing
happen' – often left out, Auden added
'poetry is a way of happening,
a mouth' – just how the picture is painted

might not matter. *It does for me.* He scans
the undergrowth, the tops of trees, the wind
from one to the other you move through time
and place. Lenses watch while he draws us in.

The Big Hawthorn in May, charcoal and white.
There's a moment when spring is full, he calls it
'nature's erection'. Let there be light
near Rudston. *Isn't that the start of it all?*

Without the brushstroke there is no pleasure.

'...A SEA THAT MAY GO ON SOME TIME'
after Alice Oswald

...where's the rose...?
        Poiesia: she overheard
a sound as of sand informing sea

sea to sand
    where?
        The tip, the dump, spilt plastic,
landfill like all their other rubbish and
    whose?

 Sand to sea
        earth men with watering cans,
desalination plant, fork, rake, hoes –

the sand puckered, begging for the sea

– earth-ruckus, rumour, rank soil, carbon
indigestion, spent uranium,
bores, grouts, rapeseed, harrows
                cover me!

Sea sounds
glass bells, sweet sanderlings' toes, neap tides

sand says
enough, come, cover me now, cover me

in under me now
              over
        we shall
mirror the fall of the final swallow

    '...*a sea that*'... is a line from Oswald's 'The three wise men of Gotham who set out to catch the moon in a net'.

LIST OF WORK 1902

'The Boiler Makers' and Iron and Steel Ship Builders Society List of Work, to come into force on and after May 1st 1902. This list is intended to avoid continual friction between Union members.'

Bilge Keels, Breast Hooks, Back Bone or Whale Back
Breakwater and Bow Chocks and Shoots
Wheel Houses, Chart Houses, and Side Houses
Companions, and circular and square Hatch Coamings
Chain Locker, Donkey Engine Seat, all Doors to casings, bunkers and houses
Tank side Plates and Bars and Brackets
Facing Plates and Angles, Tunnel and rubber Plates and Angles (except specified in Shipwrights' List)
Stool and Thrust Blocks in tunnel
Fresh-water Tanks built in vessel, Gangway Doors, Waterway Angles on all decks and Gunwale Bars
Gravits, Plates and Angles, intercostal Plates and Bars, Moulding, Hawes pipe, Stiffening Plate, all Liners and Lugs
Pipe Covers and Plate Covers for running steering gear
Rudder, single and double plated, also Bridge Plate
and Front Stanchions' Foot, Plate or Bars
Mast Steps, Plates and Bars
Tank-top Plating and Angles
Tank Lids and Wash Plates
Longitudinal Girders, Plates and Bars
Wash Port and Coal Port Doors
Ventilators and Coal Pipe Plates
Skylights and Trunks
Turtle Backs, Deck-ties and Bridles
Box-beams and Watertight Flats
Water-closet Plates and Angles
Shell-plating and Shell Liners
Lighthouse Towers and Bulwarks
Masts, Yards and Bowsprits
Mast-rings and Strength-plates
Fairlead Plates and Bars, Bulb-iron Winch Seating and Bollard Plates.

found in: A Historical Survey of the Boiler Makers' and Iron and Steel Ship Builders' Society from August 1834 to August 1904 by D.C. Cummings, General Secretary (Newcastle-on-Tyne:1905).

FROM A CHINA DIARY, 1988
for Lao Pang, my fellow traveller

Tianjin, Sept 5 EARLY LEARNING

Party and
Government

separate
and together

wu wei: willed in-
voluntary action

a State
of being

a way
of happening

it becomes us
as *Tao* was

harmony in Middle C
and minor key.

*

Tea tastes better
on second infusion

hot water

a lid on mugs
lifted only when every leaf

has sunk.

Beijing University (BEIDA), Sept 8

    This site
    contains knowledge

    within its walls
    problems lie.

    'Do Nothing
    Do Everything':

    Taoist characters
    within the Forbidden City.

    *

Ji Xian, Sept 14 'THE RESPONSIBILITY SYSTEM'

In 1981: a carter
skilled with cart and two horses.

Economic Reforms.

The village makes him a contract:
he has the cart and two horses for one year,
keeps everything he earns above 2,000 yuan.

Just one condition:

if the horses become thin
he will be fined.
Otherwise he gets a bonus at year end
based on their weight.

For nine months the carter
works the horses hard.

He earns double the 2,000 yuan
then fattens the horses up.

He asks for his bonus.

'But', the village council says,
'the bonus is so big we cannot pay
and the horses so fat they will not work.'

The council takes the carter to court.

'What about my contract?'

'What about the village?'

The county judge says,
'The village need not pay the bonus
but you, old man, can keep the horses.'

*

Wuhan, Sept 25 A HAN GIRL IN A TOWNSHIP IN SHANXI

fell in love
with a man from a National Minority.

She was treated in hospital,
her condition: 'anti-social'.

*

Wuhan, Sept 26

    'Moon cakes' — *yuebin* —
    full of fruit and spices, are eaten
    this and every September
    in the light of the harvest moon.

    In 1368 Zhu Yuazhey
    a peasant monk turned bandit
    from the South,
    had them baked in millions.

    A tocsin for rebellion
    each one contained a message:
    the people were to rise at midnight
    to overthrow the Mongol empire

    which they did.

    *

Chongqing, Sept 28 MILITARY MUSEUM

From a village wall in 1934:
'this Soviet follows the principles of the Paris Commune.'

From caves in Yenan

long marchers, peasants and workers
turn a struggle against landlords
into a war of national liberation,

see how
'soldiers help to get the harvest in.'

Photo, 1988:
Zhao Ziyang, active in the war against Japan
with, then against, the Kuomintang,
in 1938, joined the Party.

Fifty years later, Secretary General
Central Committee
Chinese Communist Party,

he says,
'A fully developed commodity economy
will take at least one hundred years:
capitalist management under socialist control –
the primary stage of socialism.'

*

Beiwenqua, Sept 30 THE VISIT

    Lao Pang is climbing the stairs:
    he has not seen his sister in ten years.

    Three week's journey from Tianjin.
    'Come in!' she laughs
    through her tears.

    Sister and brother;
    with wet and puckered eyes,
    cheeks too near to talk.

    Her lungs are weak.
    One son is mentally sick.
    Her husband has stomach cancer.

    She divides an apple between her guests
    brings tea
    puts on a tape
    turning to Pang's nieces to dance.

    A picture is taken.

    She sighs:
    'I'll never get to Tianjin.'
    Sighs again, 'letters make distance seem longer.'

    Lao Pang laughs, through his tears.

    With his fellow traveller
    he leaves for the river.

    *

On the Yangtze River, Oct 3-5

FOR WHOM IS NOW A BETTER TIME THAN THEN?

1.

For the peasant who took his tortoise
one thousand kilometres from home,
to Dong Hu Lake in Hubei province:

the lake feeds into the Yangtze.
He put the tortoise in (as is the custom)
to home, like a pigeon.

Twenty-six years later
the tortoise came home.
'This is his best so far', the peasant said,

'but he can do better.
Next time he comes home

I shall be dead.'

2.
For the Kuomintang veteran from Sichuan,
exiled to Taiwan in nineteen forty-nine,
a lifetime later back on the Yangtze.

Upriver in Sichuan he found no home:
too near the waterline, it had flooded.
His dead brother's son-in-law received him.

Down river from Hubei province to Shanghai
on one last journey through the Gorges
the old soldier said –

should his first wife not be found there –
'I shall look in Manchuria,

for that was where she came from.'

YET FRANCISCAN DON WAS NEVER MORE
HIMSELF THAN IN THIS FERTILE GLASS,
Wallace Stevens 'The Man with the Blue Guitar'

1.

Disappointed by the Vatican,
all clay and gold, damask and stone,
Brother Peter, a Franciscan mendicant

takes ship from Brindisi to Haifa,
crosses hills and deserts to find himself
alone in the Dubai Hilton.

Concierge:
'Your Revenance, or should I say Sir,
quails' eggs and ginger sorbet
on a bed of lettuce hearts?'

Brother Peter in audible prayer:
'Swimsuit water extractors, a six-star
desert ski resort and look!
The Old Guitarist. Dear God -
a blue Picasso. With my first white knot
may we celebrate poverty.'

Singing more softly
of Eros and Agape,
'I will make love
to everyone, but chastely.
While taking none,
I will be careful
to give satisfaction.'

Out loud, 'This is my body....'

Touching his second knot,
'Our vow of chastity.'

2.

Explosive. Hidden in the third -
obedience – knot
on his white cordelier.

Brother Peter places a fuse
under a napkin
among the hills and valleys
of starched linen.

Then,

'WAITER! Brother,
a light please, set this, burn this
do this, in memory of me…
this is my blood.'

White cranberry juice,
a bagel slicer
and straight from the freezer
smithereens of mountain goat.

'Antonioni, Michelangelo'
Brother Peter mutters,
'Your *Deserto Rosso*
is my Armageddon Dust.'

3.

Arrested, interrogated, extradited,
our mendicant brother is rendered to Old Abbey –
a friary serving as part of
Her Majesty's Secure Estate.

Granted a single cell,
he paces and prays, for life.

On Sundays he borrows
a Securicor (Group 4) helmet.

The visor and battery-driven visor-wiper
remind him, he says,
of Sister Clare's wimple.

Two-handed – a bishops' mitre –
he puts the helmet on,

'in case of chemical,
climatic, viral
or heavenly attack.'

LITTLE BOYS
Razo: Born 1939

August 6th, 2020 was the seventy-fifth anniversary of the dropping of the Hiroshima bomb. Anxious, pandemic days generated a poem in, for me, the unusually tight form of a rule-breaking sestina. The poem draws on my own little-boy, disjointed, teenaged and adult times, as well as on a poetic fascination with names – with what things, in this culture, get called, and why.

Little Boy was the codename given to a bomb with blast power two thousand times greater than any bomb previously dropped. From 2020 to August 2022, I fell to thinking about echoes between the 'Manhattan Project' which resulted in the Hiroshima bomb and the 9/11 (2001) double-barrelled terrorist attacks on Manhattan by the Wahhabi terrorist group Al-Qaeda, also from the air. The Wild West, gun fight nature of drones as extra-judicial instruments of revenge, does not help. He who takes the sword.

Preying on my mind while writing 'Little Boys' were the codenames for the British family of *Grand Slam, Ten Ton Tessie*, and *Earthquake* bombs, siblings of which were dropped on German cities during 1945. In 'Cobra Mist', a poem in her 2021 collection *Hiddensee*, Annie Freud wrote:

> …and even the bombs had names –
> Blue Peacock, Blue Streak, Blue Danube,
> Yellow Sun, Brown Bunny, Red Beard, Violet Club
> And were subject to stress and strain like us.

Cobra Mist was the codename for a recent Anglo-American experimental radar station at Orford Ness in Suffolk.

The plutonium bomb dropped on Nagasaki less than three days after *Little Boy*, killing forty thousand people and destroying one third of the city, was known as *Fat Man*. In 1946 an Anglo-American initiative named *Project Ruby* tested a rocket-assisted weapon known as the *Disney bomb*.

While making this poem, I wanted to memorialise a whole generation's boyhoods, taking some of the weight of what passed in those days – my lifetime – as normal: *The War*, as it was known for decades after 1945, and then (until very recently in Europe) *post-war*.

LITTLE BOYS
Sestina

Born in nineteen thirty-nine, at the age of two
this one coloured-in his *Boy's Own* book of bombs, kill
kill Hitler! Twenty million Russian lives later
lisping 'Wed' Army, he played at being
Stalin, his Dad's Jo to end the war. One terrorist
should serve, alone, to bring his hunting father home.

The Nazi-Soviet Pact abandoned in two
despotic heads, 'Mother, what's a terrorist?'
Then, 'Bwitzkwieg?' Evacuees usurped his place at home,
their books above his head. 'Our' bombers droned, to kill
all sleep, over and in his head, plus every living being
in Dresden. Called blanket or carpet bombing later.

Demob unhappy, a new suit, some months later
our boy's stoic, both-wars-weary father came back home.
His young thing swallowed pain. Whose? Who's being
displaced again, less special? 'Boy' sobs all through his two-
times table, cries out for Enid Blyton, needs to kill
Our Father Which Art... him? His Son a terrorist?

Six million murders. Jewish people need a home,
Zion, to call their own. Our British Mandate says 'later,
not yet.' In nineteen forty-six Irgun terrorists
blow up King David Hotel, their reason being
our secret *Operation Agatha*. Codenames kill:
Operation Shark. *V.3*. Father calls it 'Israel's new V.2.'

'From now on bomb will be met by bomb', *Boche* terrorist
Hitler's boast in nineteen thirty-nine. Twelve years later,
prep-school cricket, Tallboy's post war sun, Kent at home
to Sussex. No lisp now: 'Korrrea!' MacArthur, two-
then five-star General, scored this schoolboy's being:
bomb Manchuria, blockade China, go for the kill!

Our Empire Story. Mau Mau next, the nineteen-fifties too,
one thousand 'natives' hung, the question at school being
'why don't we bomb them?' Then Malaya. Crush them, kill!
'Middle class and British born', the press, years later
feigns surprise: a native British, airport terrorist-
bombing plot. East Enders? Believers? From a bad home?

Decades later, the killing fields, the *War on Terror,*
shalom, salaam being two such peaceful greetings
still sending boys away.
                      Carry them home.

NEWBORN

Chubby, caterwauling baby, filling-out
nicely, ends *previously* for ever.
Before, fat hopes. After? The hope is *please stay*.

Those first notes, semiquavers tripping
towards nearby trains, the underside of leaves,
overhead 'planes. Light-closed eyes twitch

for primal milk in spasmodic, fugal-
velociraptor, arms and legs-led moves.
A vacuum suddenly losing balance

with Big Bang. Might never have happened
all that plainsong, deep-throat music of the spheres.
Oxygen? Just in time. Aeons of breath got swallowed

before this matter of fact, this newborn.
Before the fact of this matter for crying
out loud, silence had a wound to burst.

2.

TRIBUTES AND ACHES

THANK YOU, AUDEN

We get muddled. Take your Ars Poetica,
how home-bound songs – *The Sea and the Mirror* –
make nothing happen etc etc.
But you, with Prospero, so often conjure

from Weland's Smithy, that 'cave of making',
light verse, unfolded lies (so is 'light' wrong?);
turn silence into objects, appearing
waters, vineyards; make time-altering song

in measures which, as poets can, keep time –
clock, calendar and season – save it; make
conspicuous fountains stop, formed by rhyme
rhythm and reason, sound for sense's sake.

With War, we cannot wish you stuck in London,
no longer new, just 'W. H. Auden.'
You lived to fight in Middagh St., Brooklyn,
for late stanzas *About the House*, Kirchstetten.

A poet with something to say, you thought
as well as thanked; your Prelude – *New Year Letter* –
by keeping Life in quarantine from Art,
showed how and why you'd write them down, together.

Your habitat, the body in your work
is ours. You as Goethe, puns, pre-particle
physics, the Fall, your glands…admirers shirk.
You as poet? The definite article.

Immediately apt in every metre,
you asked of any poem: does it work?
An epithalamium for Peter
and Rita must fit, like your saddle-tank lok.

Your *merle* and *mavis*, for blackbird and thrush,
was partly swank, but also to honour
George Herbert, editing his work for us:
like de la Mare an unexpected Master.

Endearments, nocturnes, epitaphs to die for,
bucolics – one for Isaiah Berlin
called 'Lakes' as long-sighted as him, saw
glints, oxbows, piedmonts, sinks, pots, moraines....

You found old words which worked, like *crankle* for bends
in streams; your nouns – *thinks, manage* – seemed homely
and even *frettolosamente* means
what the sound-sign does: it moves hurriedly.

The word of God made flesh as boy, provoked
your poem, 'The Question', in *Thank You Fog*.
Where *did* He get that extra chromosome
unless from Joseph or some preying sod?

And in 'Friday's Child': did He really break
the seal and rise again? You dared not say
you had an urgent question, 'Law like
Love'...but how to keep it, from day to day?

Things happen once and for all: a matter
of Time. Incarnation is only odd
to fallen selves like ours who cannot ever
get our tongues around It, uttering God.

In Time, nothing is settled once and for all.
These days, crucifixion is not that odd –
all over by three ('Nones') most days – for all
who look to follow the Lamb of God.

You knew about suffering: how mercy
pity, peace and love find blood on the hands
of holy diggers in God's Just City
and wide-eyed builders in new-found lands.

Imp? Yes, you dared to trace your singing back
to source: a baby cuckolding brothers
in clefts and gurgles of water and rock
in limestone, what could be more like Mother?

Her Ariel, so clever with such simple
words, like *abject* for that (weeping?) willow,
or *senile* for the wide, alluvial
plains old rivers make from bloated meadows.

'Out on the lawn,' however memorable
that summer was, you cut from one Selection;
you warned against the definite article.
'The sounded note is the restored relation'

you put in prose, on stage as Henry James,
in case we thought it *your* suggestion
that Verbal Numbers, lyric, sol-fa games
restore our oldest, dumb relations.

In *For the Time Being*, 'Joseph is me'.
His jealousy of Mary, yours of Kallman
ran through your longer, less-read poetry:
an island of un-set sound. Look! Caliban –

he, Chester Kallman, stood you up; genius
of marriage, Eros to Agape, you
confused his coming with that of Jesus,
the One Big Word, a heresy. You knew.

Your grace note, 'dear', your Prince disrobed, your chum
the object of your endless artistry
fine words, forgiving music, painful fun
and, whisper it in Latin, charity.

As fallen creatures loving falling leaves
we munch necessity, spit out freedom,
we love our neighbours, sometimes, as ourselves
and mind, or not, the life of other kingdoms.

Mother's boy, undressed in print already –
Achilles? Not the hirsute type – you sang
(forget the private poems) impossibly
of love too small, unwilled and Anglican.

For you, love was better out of legend,
as finite, human, simplest love. Then love
lost, disenchanted, as passive gerund,
in the end, a state of grace, love as love.

Not Tristan's love (for Mark, you thought, not Her)
or Juliet's passion – that will to lie –
but love of each minute particular,
we must love one another or (and?) die.

MEDITATION IN UNSEASONAL HAIKU

Now is anytime.
My past, if it's mine. Future
dawns, as cocks crow.

Here is anywhere
eye-side of the camera.
Home, as the crow flies.

We is simply a string bag
Everyone, but
as things stand, half full.

We, here, now, alive.
Animal, vegetable
and yes, mineral.

Could *we* be all this,
dispersing Greeks and Trojans,
such herds, sods, and clumps?

Can *here* be where we
live? Might Odysseus stay
to fight his corner?

Can *now* go on and
on, with Orpheus singing
and no turning back ?

We, Here, Now but not
yet: a meditation,
all we need to know.

PASSION FLOWER

Nectar flowers
open at night disappear
in the morning.

Subgenus
passiflora trisecta
bat pollinated,

habitat
high altitude areas
of Peru and Bolivia.

Trifoliate leaves in
supersection tasconia
have a velvet pubescence.

SISTER
FUTURE PERFECT

Lesions. The cold teabags left
films of blue, then brown
in concentrates of mud
where the cup was.

Long afternoon, late tea.
August itself.
Deliberately she said,
'as good a place as any.'

We watched the clematis,
its solo, purple horn –
fish, blood and bone-meal fed –
cling stubbornly to day,

no calyx or coronae.
My sister talked in silences
awkwardly grafted,
all tendrils and stamens.

'Ten letters. Agapanthus.
Look how dry they are,'
she said. 'I'm not very good at God.'
I said, 'Nine across. Metastases?'

INCARNATION, IN FIVE REGISTERS

And whoever is mov'd by Faith *to assent to it, is conscious of a continued Miracle in his own Person, which subverts all the Principles of his Understanding, and gives him a Determination to believe what is most contrary to Custom and Experience.*
      David Hume, 'Of Miracles'

What time?

was that One? Dare we say 'incarnation'?
Would repetition really help? At this…

the unlikely improbable begot
the definite article, in the flesh

in time out of mind. What's that? Half time, full
or extra time, warp, bubble, once upon a….

Too many question-marks, look at them: *???*
Incomplete light bulbs, hotel coat hooks.

For this happenstance, 'time' is too
straight. It straggles, thickens with thyme.

Here and gone

the bumbarrels in uncountable numbers –
long-tailed tits – materialise as one.

Alight is hardly the word, they tilt
air to apple, maple to ash, nowhere

still or – blink – still there, visible to seers
who twitch to tell the world the time and place.

Long-tailed males have more than one lover,
finches and wagtails sometimes join the flock.

When God made (was made?) flesh, what was flesh made?
Cuckold, a rib or rack of lamb – or God?

A real

concert performance. Too beautiful
not to be true. Complete illusion.

Undoubtedly Thomas, the trouble is
we never know what to do with it.

George Puttenham in 1589
on paralipsis, 'as when we will not

seem to know a thing and yet we know it
well enough.' We feel it in our bones, freeze

too too solid, too full of it to know
how to be Hamlet, 'unpregnant of our cause'.

B'Jesus

What did he know beyond Himself? His tree,
the family forest, deep mythologies

of boats, the Corn King, snakes and ladders, Zeus,
the old gods' carryings on, from Ovid?

Then Shakespeare. He clearly knew that nothing
has to be; that counsel hardly ever works;

that transformations always happen;
and sacrifice often is The End.

Who am I? Thou sayest it. Trinity?
The third person was part of his grammar.

Incarnation

'My son'. Can anyone without one weigh
these words, less likely than anything else?

Resurrection? It happens every night,
Though still I die, I live again still longing.

Nothing *is* except in relation
to something or other, some body else.

Nothing falls, but into categories
imposed by us, with more than one sense

including God who, Immanuel,
is inconceivable unless through us.

SHAKESCENE

Authority, that stuff – its Dukes and Kings
First Lords and Second, ensigns, underlings –
you put on stage as puff, *honour, trim reckoning*
in feathers which wear out, something of nothing
out-sung by Fools in songs and syllogisms
for king crows banishing, tonguing, blinding
followers beyond their worst imagining.

Hey ding a ding ding while millions feed on
nothing, we lovers love to sing.
From nowhere we come, to no one we cling
except each others' fear of others lying
where we've lain receiving love – us groundlings
relishing your games with words. *Music, do I hear*
poetry *unlimited*, to make kings panic?
                               Lights, Ho! Lights.

INVITATION TO A DEAD-HEADING

Coming across them in the park
I knew they belonged to this plot,
bevy, collect, recitative,
sheaf and seminar of poets.

Common
good in bunches and in clumps
grounded to suggest movement
silently indicating sound.
Easy to like, impossible to grasp
deliberately burying their origins.

Instructions:
plant in loam
three times as deep as the length of a bulb
to help them naturalise
and stop them going blind

as Tenor or Ground?
Metaphor yes but
unfortunately also Spring,
unusable except as metal
and as dangerous in English verse
as shards and mirrors and Me.

Once upon a time
punctual, wild, eponyms
caught the sun
like brass bands in April weather

but now many-layered petals,
cornucopias, irregular, narcissistic,
some shy, some priapic,
exist as cultivars of modern –
Write it! –
daffodils.

WHERE THERE ONLY EVER IS

Where there only ever is old wood
scaffolding and architectural salvage,
through the perfect hollowness of empty
fennel stalks, my heart went out this summer
to dry, regimented, once upon a time
bedding plants under crumbling limestone walls

and to ugly old magnolia leaves
brown and bark-brittle, which
unlike other leaves on less archaic trees
will never nurse or even touch
the little finger, gnome's hat bandages
which are next summer's curled-up cotton,
sometimes succulent, more often dead
furled-umbrella buds.

HOW ARE WE SUPPOSED TO SING?

> ... *it's a bloody*
> *tempest out there*
> *how are we supposed to sing?*
> from Philip Gross | Lesley Saunders
> *A Part of the Main* (2018)

1. With Amaryllis

Little time left, few listeners, Amaryllis
at long last shares her wherewithal, sings one
seemingly endless song. From the top of a long stem
she flowers, as if for ever makes another
if we're lucky another, up to twelve the same
audible colour. No makeup needed, her name
is enough: Amaryllis. Play it again Ama

your subfamily *Amaryllidoideae* has a touch
of bitterness, with amaro embracing Mary.
Ama, mother, this cultivar of the true lily
is sometimes known as belladonna, gilded lady
symbolic of pride and pastoral poetry.
Full of make-believe – deae – a goddess no doubt:
a ma ryl li doi deae plays on her syllables

a melody, but also a story of blood:
an early unrequited crush, Amaryllis
on Alteo. Mythology has her singing
in the woods, in eclogues and idylls a nymph
become shepherd, in love with handsome Alteo.
He was cold, seldom looked up, could only love flowers.
When she asked, what did the oracle propose?

Nothing as modern as meanings or thin, like opinion.
In those days Delphi traded in destiny,
unsqueamish, sacrificial saws. Amaryllis in Greek
means to sparkle, catch the light. So she was to cut herself,
pierce her heart with a golden arrow – her white flowers
retain their crimson veins – visit Alteo's cottage
every day, shedding drops of blood along the way.

It worked. On the thirtieth day red, funnel-shaped
pheromonic flowers began to bloom, each drop
a seed-cum-bulb. Nowadays – given six weeks' summer
rest in a cool dark place – Amaryllis bulbs
easily outlive all husbandmen. Alteo
was love-struck, our hero's heart was healed, leaving us
a contested genus, *Hippeastrum*
                                    to sing along with.

2. And with lettuce, *Lactuca Sativa*

Seasons ago, Amaryllis. Three long months later
lettuces: cut and come again, cos, crisphead, butterhead
green or red Romaine, looseleaf, Longstreath's Earliest, Eichling's
(eighteen seventy-three) Early Market, a type called stem
Asparagus lettuce, Lollo Rosso, Little Gem
Iceberg, All Year Round cultivars sing while Amaryllis
whose name is a song, gets potted – mainly for carols at Christmas

in terracotta. Playing on words for common or garden
if antiscorbutic things, is itself to sing, even in Latin.
Lactuca , milk-white latex oozing from cut stems
while *sativa* means sown, fingered-in, featured for thousands
of years in Eastern plots. So forty-five day full size
curly-leaf Longstreath's has sobriquets: Long Stander, Forcing
White, Earliest Cutting, Black-seeded Simpson's heirloom

lettuce. Seeds sown lightly with granules of dry volcanic
rock called Perlite allow for singular lockdown song
waited for, watered, potted on, pricked out, for Anglo Saxons
sleepwort, a narcotic, for Ancient Egyptians symbolic
of sexual prowess, profane for Iraqui Yazidis'
eyes down with Alteo's. Greek tales go back from lactuca
to nectar, death, yet another handsome youth and wilting

funeral gardens with beds laid out for Adonis, that legend
for looking good and being loved – uncontrollably –
in under- and overworld tales. In Greek myth erotic's not it
but incest is, and loves with lyrical names: Aphrodite,
Persephone, Venus, mother Myrrha, a resinous tree.
One day Adonis, out hunting, died in Aphrodite's arms
gored by a pig's tusk. His blood sweetened the soil to sire

anemones: windflowers. With such a name why sing on
with salad? Because, like visiting gods as All-Saviours,
lettuces come quickly, get picked or shoot, die, go flaccid.
So Sappho sings of mourning midsummer maidens making
Adonis Gardens, full of withered fennel and lettuce
floated, with chanting and recitative, far out to sea.
Nowadays, lettuce is just one of the daisies
                              an *Asteraceae.*

THE VIOLET RAY MACHINE
(price £4/15/0)

*exhibited at the Wembley Great Exhibition of 1923,
advertised to have a 'wonderful effect' on the following diseases:*

Abscess, Acne Vulgaris, Alcohol and Drug Habits, Arthritis Deformans, Asthenopia, Asthma, Alexia, Atrophy of the Optic Nerve, Baldness, Bladder Disease, Blood Pressure, Boils, Brain Fag, Breast Development, Bronchitis, Bruises, Bunions, Burns, Callouses and Corns, Cancer, Carbuncle, Cataract, Colds and Catarrh, Catarrh of Womb, Chapped Hands and Face, Chilblains, Cold Extremities, Colitis, Constipation, Corneal Opacity, Dandruff, Deafness, Diabetes, Dropsy, Dyspepsia, Earache and Eardiseases, Eczema, Fistula, Freckles, Frost Bites, Goiter, Gout, Grey Hair, Gripe, Hay Fever, Headache, Hives and Rash, Hardening of the Arteries, Hemorrhoids, Hypertension, Impotence, Infantile Paralysis, Insomnia, Intraocular Hemorrhage, Iritis, Leucorrhea, Lumbago, Massage, Menstruation, Mumps, Nervousness, Neuralgia, Neuritis, Obesity, Pains, Paralysis, Piles, Pleurisy, Pneumonia, Rheumatism, Scars, Skin Disease, Sore Feet, Stone Bruises, Sciatica, Sore Throat, Throat Diseases, Stiff Neck and Joints, Tonsillitis, Uric Acid conditions, Warts.

found in the Woolstaplers' Museum, Chipping Camden

TIME TO MOVE ON

Before him hermits
but ever since Blake
Romantics
only not John Clare
saw fit to inhabit
the rough split second
for longer than anyone else.

Harvesting its sadness
which they called gladness
they held it up with a rhyme.
Beating its bounds
they pecked at its passing
holding it down with a foot
like powerful owls with a rat.

APPRENTICE POET: LEARNING TO GET LOST WITHOUT ANXIETY

At First

She could not say *possibility* without
letting in the likelihood it might not
must not, cannot, will not and will happen right
on cue. Endlessly possible: the brunt
of its infinite evanescence. So she leaves out
y-words like *simultaneity* for all at
onceness. Avoids these tut-tut *t*s, omits
abstractions, *-nesses*, as well as *-shuns*. Angst
came unsolicited, toxic. Her soul-self then
asked, why don't you, with your one (lost) reader, dispense
with it? Use all six senses, unravel
rococo prosodic entanglements,
end one sonnet here. Impatient poets
tack away in elegant, well-wrought couplets.

Then

All at sea, lost, our poet drops anchor
in an ocean of black lit by pinpricks of silver
light. Cormorants cluster. Her soul-self allows her
to feel singular shoals she longs to find words for.
She puts out long lines, one after another
letting go of each hesitant comma.
Phishing? Punning? Simile? Metaphor?
It's the *unlikes* inside her she longs to offer:
things with – not displacing – *ideas* whose
entangled tales her poems could never quite
gut: cod, coelacanth, squid, thornback skate
incipient whitebait which dragnets lose.
Festina lente, she sails on slowly
learning to get lost, composing anxiety.

And then

a 'wake' of black and white Palm-nut vultures
warns her (where from?) to dispense with designs
on 'the reader'. A little bird tells her
where waters meet to rhyme, rehearse fine names:
the Balearic or Sooty Shearwater
the Stormy Petrel in wave-skimming flight
one Black Guillemot with flashes of white
noise, like signals from eavesdropping matter
or rap from a Latin band she loved, *Poesia
Acústica*. Beside herself now, her *anima*
Other lets go of gender, capital letter
vocative O and histrionic Lo!
Next to harpooning Common or Arctic Terns
she's alone with her soul-self, addressee unknown.

A CHRISTMAS GOSPEL

Between ourselves
we conceive the world:
unmake, make, unmake
this and that.

Down to earth we marry
hell to heaven.

Perish the thought
of God the Father
which we uttered in
the first place.

Without life, in which
god lives, moves and
catches Her breath
was not anything made that was made.

His beginning
was our word.

By god
I
could not begin
or even blink at the eye of God

until *hodie*, when
one erupting fact
bled into each and every fantasy.

It became *Us*
but becomes *and*...

that's quite enough
to be getting on with.

INSTRUCTIONS FROM *LOS*
(Blake's prophetic other)

Reach
    for linked fountains
    inside your heads,
    imaginal unities.

Fight
    crazed wars, against
    bone-hard seeming Fact
    construct Golgonooza.

Dissolve
    salt mud in runnels,
    like lugworms
    perfecting fine coils of sand.

Power
    has Reasons,
    brass manacles
    of Ratiocination.

Jerusalem?
    not yet, but
    my City
    of Art and Manufacture.

POETRY
after Marianne Moore

I too, dislike it: there are things that are important beyond all this fiddle
  '… imaginary gardens with real toads in them…'

Among the many facets of identity
is habit, put on long before we came to know
all this fiddle. Let it be, let it be.

Habitus: the sea. Prehistoric fish from many
million years ago, still swimming. Lately known
among the many faces of identity

as genus *coelacanthus*. Nice categories
admit surprise: taxonomy, just so?
All such fiddle, let it be, let it be.

But *ideas* like 'fishiness'? Out of water, essences
never couple, withdraw when asked to grow
into the faces we call identity.

Whereas real *things* in green, imaginary seas,
backboned not filleted, allowed to breathe,
all such fiddle, let it be, let it be

as toad-like as a toad, as ugly as Adonis,
cold-blooded matter, lungs on legs, bendable bones.
Among so many facets of identity
all those fiddles already are: poetry.

A PART OF SPEECH?

Abbá, father...

Not Dad but maybe Mum's the word for reticence
the silence to which Christ cried out in pain.

Absent: white noise or any intervention.

Was there some element of verb, of
absént, that unstressed stress? God, but here and now?

Colloquial, like *being as how*?

Silence as abject, held between coequal
emphases: subject withholds, doesn't object.

The phantom belonging of a missing limb.

FRESH GREEN SAP

An old saw says
you fall in love easily,
off a log.

He fell for her,
felled at first sight.

She fell for a
baby, head over
heels in love.

On Scafell
they leapt into love

felt sore, saw, felt,
left deciduous trees

followed a stream
found a fresh spring
took off his gold ring.

At seventeenth sight
they climbed into love
up at the Pike.

Heels above
head for love

she sawed at a branch
of the pine
to which he had clung -

Love's teeth cut.

3.

LIST AND FOUND
NOW AND THEN

FOLIE DE GRANDEUR
from and to Greta Thunberg

No one
is too small
to make
a difference.

No one
is too big
not to make
much difference.

PAINTER
(for F.M.)

1.

In fallow years, using empty seaside shells
she overheard a hidden garden: quiet and distant.
Learning how to cook, the children could not see it
while she picked up pale blue Canterbury Bells.

Beside herself, what was she doing buying loads
of garden-centre strawberries, out of place alpines,
while a dull red, one-man, lumbering combine
tractor went by, giant tyres cutting up her road?

2.

In lockdown, she started painting harvests,
eye, heart and hand out of her mind. Golden yellow
for maize, delft-blue flax, pockets of pink-red mallow,
corncrakes on green-and-white buckwheat, full forests

in oils, people – whole villages - coming and going,
some scything, some stooking, drinking or sleeping.
She learned how to go on working, seizing
full moons for reaping late-seasonal sowing.

IN-
HABITED

'The Lord's' was a prayer my generation learned by rote,
so its cadences lodged deep inside

God in all of us, re-
membered be your name.

Our re-
public come,
our wills be one
for all,
and all for one

Here
Today

we will
grow, reap, grind, knead, bake, then slice
our daily bread.

Trespasses?
The measure for mercy is ours:
we ask for no more than we give.

Temptation?
Lead us not to strip
the evil which goes with good in 'us'
and stick it onto 'them'.

For ours is the human condition
fleshed out
with power in our stories

of Now.
again and again
Amen.

AN ILLICIT ACHE,
FATHER FOR SON

I feel it in my gums, in the down
on my arms, but definitely not in the
heart's flutter, or thud. No anticipation,
just *missing*: bone-hard, animal, sensory
loss, laid down – undertaken – long ago.

You know how long *my* father and mother
have been dead: it's blood. You will say 'no'
but when I go, soon now my son, you will savour
the ache, the gap where a tooth never was.
You may taste it as air on the tip of your tongue.

Flesh of my flesh, it's nothing personal.
It almost doesn't matter who we are
or what who did wrong – taken from the fridge
grief can turn out quite tasty. Left on the bone
pain can be – I have to say already is – for me

on occasion, rather rewarding.

PARENTHESIS
for H.E.Y.

The elms grew fewer before he died.
Rapacious farmers – war profiteers – unhedged
and ditched the empty landscape where he lived.
Winter-sweet – his favourite – gave out scent
at half-inch intervals from wooden stems –
a splash of bitters, crimson, in wax-like
flowers. *All the perfumes of Arabia*
he said most weekends, nursing gentians
whose blue horns, among the granite, gave out none.
He took his pleasures separate. Two wars.
The First against *the Hun,* stopped him. One son
married a German, the other a Jew.
Later in the spring, when the leaves came,
who could say who, or what, was promoted?

ON READING *EZEKIEL* IN 2021-2

Foreseen, told in the name of One not
(yet) born again, jealous, importunate God
landlord for His People: *Israel* has no need
or want to wander, will have found a plot
to till and tell in less than honeyed words.
Commanded, covenanted, script in stone,
their ark and brood are theirs to have and hold –
with every modern ploughshare beaten into swords.

Uttered: come to pass, Outsiders, Othered, look
on Zion: glass-eyes turn on Gaza. No settlement,
but a strip – of what? Palestine? From *peleshet*,
a Hebrew (and Egyptian) word for folks
who roll on, pass under to over, conquer
old-new lands? Israel fought Judah, wants 'Judea-
Sumeria'. What's in a name? 'Arabia'?
That fantasy: a uni- not our polyverse.

Big name, *Jove*, for the nameless one *Jehovah*.
I exhale *h* to breathe *Yah Weh* and say –
as a creature whose wordless way to pray
is breath – *Oh my God, O Yah Weh*.
Progenitor of Adam whose name means 'earth':
if, in the beginning, all of us came from One
how come we cannot let an Other in?
Breathe with me breath of God: bread, way, tree, staff
    of Life.

NOW AND THEN
from a son (1939 -) to a mother (1908-1997)

Whereas Now is our best and only hope
of forever, as we rummage to find
the famous grain of sand, forever
is forever
           on autopilot. It cuts
both ways:
           a black dog, shaking its pelt
out from under drops of silver water
following a swim, instantly forgotten
in the flat fullness of a slow river.

'Is it today Stephen?' my mother would ask
time after immemorial time
out of mind, always afternoon. 'Only?'
If only
     only could ever be alone
like Then:
           'Not now my boy, do keep still!' When
or whose engorged ache was that? Mine
– the adult son's, an infant in arms –
or any mother's pain in nineteen thirty-nine?

ENDEARMENTS
I love you O Lord, David, Psalm 18.

1.

I love You but
'Luv Yer
        mwah, byee…'?

Here is the *shipping news*
(by now our island prayer)
cyclonic four or five
occasionally six later….
are litanies what You like?

In the end, Prospero
threw away his wand.
Christians think it wasn't his
 – or ours – to have: mere alchemy.
Creator Shakespeare used his gift
lightly, immortality? in *writing!*
Loue labours wonne got lost, so
Jack hath not Jill.

In love with love
yeah, yeah, pluck the lyre
for Jesus: *Jesu my desire.*
A coiled snake God
awaits me. I, his little charmer?

2.

You love me but
God is …
        is love?

If You, quite simply, are –
if being is what You do –
can You be one thing
or another, leave alone
one thing after another?

God as subject noun –
a single part of speech –
governs each and any verb.
But takes a single object: *moi?*
love? what about hate? or pyjamas?
At all events, the verb 'to be'
belongs to Sanskrit *bhu*,
which meant: 'to grow'.

    Noun verb, verb noun,
    object subject, subject object.
    Is was Word, *was* is God
    uttered once. No silver thruppence
    in that plum pudding.

3.

Is love the thing
or some
       thing else,

another idiom? But
not *Lord* mi'lud, or lady –
my lord, a hunchback (ob.)
from lordosis (med.) –
and not metaphor, not like…

like anything
unless everything
which means nothing
under the sun.
What tense? Plu- or future perfect?
We keep telling you, you made us
in Your own image, speaking likenesses.
You like us, we like you,
the dead spit

    … of what? Full of self-pity,
milk and honey, the Psalmist
David knew. I don't. But cannot end:
You that way, we this way
            [*Exeunt*]
or say Adieu, we'll be alright without you.

HIS DAUGHTER TO HER DAUGHTER, 'GRANDFATHER' REMEMBERED

With you he talked grownup. You want him back.
But your grandfather lived on another planet
acting out everything he longed for most,
was kindness itself, lovely no doubt, but
what is it to *botanise on asphalt*
trudge whole days *deep down riverbeds*
no boots, on a map, alone in his shed?
You can conjure him now, dancing with words
present-tensing the past, future-perfecting
a need to explain: *that's not what I said.*

THOUGH HE COULD

Though he could likely
be made so, to serve
a *huis clos*, tight knit
out-of-sorts system's
whirring, he's not yet
mad or ill.

He has one supple
self, a briar or dog
wild and wandering
rose, aching for garden
husbandry. Fetching,
becoming

what he and she, they,
me, you, I, us all
need now to be: ordinary
as hell where heaven
is, to common ourselves
peer to peer, to

lie down with lions
as lambs. Our burnt offerings
done, sunny side down.
In endist times at
four score years and ten,
terminal.

MUSE TO POET

*To what
purpose dost thou
hoard thy words?*

I like
copious storms,
no alibis,

you move
bits of hard sense
scored pebble stones

from head to page.

I sniff
night-scented stock
floodplain as metaphor,

you keep
one of your eyes
asquint from mine

as *hawk on bough.*

Why not try
a dance in step
our two tongues prodigal?

The lines in italics are from William Shakespeare's *Richard II* and Robert Browning's *A Woman's Last Word.*

'god'

Not a bit of this
and that, but tarmac
vapour-trail, sky bandage.
Every *where?*
Everything *else.*
This tuft, that star,
among and between
in here over there,
without membrane
or integument

Apostrophe '
belongs to,
omitted, something
someone once said.
Stories in which
word was only
the beginning, when
with went with *was.*
Still is...Happens....
I did...It might....

Plural? Probably not
A pro- or abstract noun.
An *assembly?*
Emily Dickinson thought so.
Present continuous,
plu- as well as future perfect.
A *num* question, expecting
the answer No and
 a regular verb
of the first conjugation

amo amas amat

COMPLICATIONS

*the sheer complications of relations that hover
on the borderlines of class and persona,* Richard Cobb, Still Life (1983)

I do feel awkward
on a Friday morning
when we have company
or I'm writing at home
how spotless it all looks.

Meet Mags? Margaret? She,
she *what*? Helps, comes round, *does*,
lives in the village, cleans?
Is a conversation
supposed to start, a chat?
A friend just told me
her Mum cleaned, no, *did*
for a 'career woman',
a 'professional'.

The going rate round here?
Weeks off unpaid? Our bed,
the boys'? Who should make them?
Easier once, when Mother
liked to read *The Lady*.

She had a *daily* 'Mrs
Mop', a village woman,
a *comfortable body*, all apron.
In charge, she knew how things work.
On-line nowadays, they bring their own
bleach, buckets, coffee,
dusters. Two at a time,
in, out. Works out cheaper
all part of a contract.

So I'm beginning to think
of an enterprise, a start-up.
Help migrant families
sort out settled status,
work with ex-offenders?

Money in their pockets.
Call it a mutual,
a Social Business:
www.
cha cha char, Bring Polish
To Your Home! My only
worry: I don't want Mags
to know how I'm thinking.
She's a family friend.

ANOTHER ACHE,
SON FOR FATHER

Black and white words
were all I had.

Can I come over?

I went to his place
to refuse my father's story.

He said,
What can I get you?

We talked.

All I had were stories
most of which I could not know.

His terrace filled,
the old man poured out wine.

I went on talking,
to a babble of welcomed guests.

Decanters shone, collecting sun
'till dusk came down.

It's time to settle our account, I said.
Then stood, as if to play his part.

Indoors, a keyboard sang.
My father smiled to the crows' feet of his eyes,

and so did I, lips, cheeks,
front teeth.

If music be...
He loved old quotes.

I finger the veins on his garden table -
marble-topped.

His life stays green with the sound of people
coming and going

looking out for me.

EPITHALAMIUM

For

the lovers
as
each other

sing
him, her
they were two.

His mother, sister,
wife, still-born daughter
come back to him.

Her brother-person,
teacher too –
her lover,

no father
but
her Other.

Hymn
her him
a single song

sung
one by
One.

GRANDFATHER

This morning's
small affairs

bypassed
lunch time.

A would-be
afternoon

disappeared
at ten-past three.

Evening:
nothing much

happening.
Such and such

will occur.
For anything

to be there or

not to exist,
some other-thing

does, which he
may never know.

LOVER, AGAIN

1.

Hazel, you turn tears to
waterfalls
staying as you do
between my eyes.

I lived there once myself, but
farmed small streams.

A neighbour was a friend to
each of us
knowing as she did
instinctively

that things were not so simple
as they seemed.

2.

She bid us luck
with such a strong "farewell"
fetching as we left
a Christmas cactus

whose leaves wait
limp and dry.

Cowslips were the first to
catch our breath
showing as we knelt
damp ochre dots.

In time we found a field
where orchids grow.

YES, BUT…
after Thelonious Monk

Yes

being beloved
objectively,
knowing that it is thus,
is

singular delight.

One
determinate drop, in

the oceanic indeterminacy of the human voice.

But

humming along,
writing it down,
so that it – makes some sense,
makes

multiple burdens.

In-
significant weights, on your

kaleidoscopic changes of tone.

ENVOI

The mistake he made
was not to write
but to think, much too much
not to write when it rained
but to think
his ordinary thoughts were poems
not to touch.

NOTES AND DEBTS

PERSEVERA – PERSEVERA – PERSE | | VERA *p.7*

Thank you to Amanda Woolley and her late, bell-ringing mother and father for the 'Persevera' motto which heads the title page of *Among the bells, the ringing career written by himself of the Rev. F.E. Robinson M.A. vicar of Drayton Berks, Master of the Oxford Diocesan Guild (c.1909)*, from which I developed the Lists and Founds of this poem. And to Alice Oswald for her Introduction to Sir Thomas Wyatt, Poems Selected by Alice Oswald (Faber and Faber, 2008).

PLASMA *p.10*

Plasma was first described by Irving Langmuir in the 1920s and has functions and a physics – and could provoke a poetry – all of its own. A 'gas' composed of ions, plasma has been described as the fourth state of matter, distinct from the other three: solids, liquids and gases. Plasma consists of atoms which have some of their orbital electrons removed, and free electrons which can move independently of each other.

LITTLE BOYS Razo *p.28*

Thank you to Fiona Sampson for this learned word. In Old Occitan ra'zu meant 'cause', 'reason', hence occasion for, a troubadour song. So the *razo* was a short piece of Occitan prose detailing the circumstances surrounding a troubadour composition. Hence my use of this lovely word to head my prose prelude to the would-be sestina which follows.

THANK YOU AUDEN *p.34*

This poem forced its way out because of Don Paterson, 'The Lyric Principle: Part 1: The Sense of Sound and Part 2: The Sound of Sense',in *Poetry Review* , Summer & Autumn 2007.

Paterson's provocations are evident, I hope, in my poem, including: his brave theorisation of lyric, language, words, and time; his plea for poetry as thinking/ telling as well as displaying/ showing; his un-Saussurian linguistics (words as 'sound-signs'); his notion of the human 'fall' into language, quite different, of course, from Auden's Augustinian theology; and his sense, shared with Auden, of a deep, lyric impulse in humans to get back behind any notion of any Fall; and to <u>contribute</u> to the making and re-making of language itself; language as a would-be 'natural object'; and, finally Paterson's rich idea of One Big Word.

My own borrowings and near-borrowings from Auden are too many to be acknowledged on the face of the poem. So I kept them to: italics for book titles and particular Auden words, inverted commas for the titles or first lines of individual poems, and to other inverted commas only where the fact of quotation seemed important to the sense of a stanza.

PASSION FLOWER *p.39*

Derived from the titles of pictures/prints of varieties of passion flower in a Royal Horticultural Society exhibition in the RHS Halls in Vincent Square.

INCARNATION IN FIVE REGISTERS *p.41*

Thank you to: Jonathan Rée, for *Witcraft: The Invention of Philosophy in English* (Allen Lane, 2019) p.191 where the David Hume epigraph comes from; Philip Gross for his poem 'Thirty Seconds on the Baltic' for 'dare we say incarnation?'; John Clare for 'bumbarrel' as the Northamptonshire name for the long-tailed tit; Anon. for *The Art of English Poesie* (1589) thought to be by George Puttenham; Richard Crashaw for his poem 'A Song (of Divine Love)' for 'though still I dy....'. And Immanuel was Kant's name too.

SHAKESCENE *p.46*

It was Robert Greene, a resentful rival and (maybe) drinking companion of Shakespeare's in London who taunted him as 'Shakescene' and as 'a crow in false feathers'. It was in Sonnet 87 that Shakespeare played with *-ing* words with the virtuosity that Greene envied.

INVITATION TO A DEAD-HEADING *p.47*

Write it/ Disaster is, famously, how Elizabeth Bishop ends her poem, 'The Art of Losing'.

ENDEARMENTS *p.71*

In *The Shape of the Dance* (2009) p.36, Michael Donaghy suggested that 'am' and 'is' share a root with the Sanskrit *asmi*, meaning to breathe. From the 17th through to the 20th century, hunchbacks were sometimes addressed as *my lord* perhaps from the Greek 'lordos'. 'Lordos' is a medical term for forward curvature of the spine. 'You that way; we this way' *Exeunt* are the final words and stage direction of Love's Labours Lost.

HIS DAUGHTER TO HER DAUGHTER *p.74*

I took 'botanising on asphalt' from Walter Benjamin's, Arcades Project. This *Passagenwerk* was written between 1927 and 1940 and unfinished when Benjamin died.

YES, BUT *(the Thelonious Monk poem) p.85*

Thank you Jonathan Rée for 'oceanic indeterminacy'.

BV - #0041 - 290124 - C0 - 216/138/5 - PB - 9781914151767 - Gloss Lamination